ANNABEL LEE

To Bernard, my father, thank you

© 1987, Gilles Thibault, illustrations

Published in Canada by Tundra Books, Montreal, Quebec H3G 1R4   Published in the United States by Tundra Books of Northern New York, Plattsburgh, NY 12901

Distributed in France, Belgium and Switzerland by Liaison Internationale

Canadian Cataloguing in Publication Data: Poe, Edgar Allan, 1809-1849. Annabel Lee. ISBN 0-88776-200-X. I. Tibo, Gilles, 1951- II. Title. PS2606. A1 1987 811'.3 C87-090098-6

The publisher has applied funds from its Canada Council block grant for 1987 toward the editing and production of this book.

Color separations and printing: Prolith Inc., Montreal   Printed in Canada

19.95   13.57

ANNABEL LEE

The poem: Edgar Allan Poe

The artist: Gilles Tibo

1798

Tundra Books

It was many and many a year ago,
  In a kingdom by the sea

That a maiden there lived, whom you may know
  By the name of Annabel Lee;

And this maiden she lived with no other thought
  Than to love and be loved by me.

_I_ was a child and _she_ was a child,
  In this kingdom by the sea,

But we loved with a love that was more than love —
 I and my Annabel Lee —
With a love that the winged seraphs of heaven
 Coveted her and me.

And this was the reason that, long ago,
   In this kingdom by the sea,
A wind blew out of a cloud, chilling
   My beautiful Annabel Lee;

So that her highborn kinsmen came
  And bore her away from me,
To shut her up in a sepulcher
  In this kingdom by the sea.

The angels, not half so happy in heaven,
  Went envying her and me —
Yes! — that was the reason (as all men know,
  In this kingdom by the sea)
That the wind came out of the cloud by night,
  Chilling and killing my Annabel Lee.

But our love it was stronger by far than the love
  Of those who were older than we —
  Of many far wiser than we —
And neither the angels in heaven above,
  Nor the demons down under the sea,
Can ever dissever my soul from the soul
  Of the beautiful Annabel Lee:

For the moon never beams, without bringing me dreams
   Of the beautiful Annabel Lee;
And the stars never rise, but I feel the bright eyes
   Of the beautiful Annabel Lee:

And so, all the night-tide, I lie down by the side
Of my darling — my darling — my life and my bride,
   In the sepulcher there by the sea —
   In her tomb by the sounding sea.